D1607350

COOL CATS

Balinese

by Betsy Rathburn

BELLWETHER MEDIA · MINNEAPOLIS, MN

Note to Librarians, Teachers, and Parents:

Blastoff! Readers are carefully developed by literacy experts and combine standards-based content with developmentally appropriate text.

Level 1 provides the most support through repetition of high-frequency words, light text, predictable sentence patterns, and strong visual support.

Level 2 offers early readers a bit more challenge through varied simple sentences, increased text load, and less repetition of high-frequency words.

Level 3 advances early-fluent readers toward fluency through increased text and concept load, less reliance on visuals, longer sentences, and more literary language.

Level 4 builds reading stamina by providing more text per page, increased use of punctuation, greater variation in sentence patterns, and increasingly challenging vocabulary.

Level 5 encourages children to move from "learning to read" to "reading to learn" by providing even more text, varied writing styles, and less familiar topics.

Whichever book is right for your reader, Blastoff! Readers are the perfect books to build confidence and encourage a love of reading that will last a lifetime!

This edition first published in 2018 by Bellwether Media, Inc.

No part of this publication may be reproduced in whole or in part without written permission of the publisher. For information regarding permission, write to Bellwether Media, Inc., Attention: Permissions Department, 5357 Penn Avenue South, Minneapolis, MN 55419.

Library of Congress Cataloging-in-Publication Data

Names: Rathburn, Betsy, author.
Title: Balinese / by Betsy Rathburn.
Description: Minneapolis, MN : Bellwether Media, Inc., 2018. | Series: Blastoff! Readers. Cool Cats | Includes bibliographical references and index. | Audience: Ages 5 to 8. | Audience: Grades K to 3.
Identifiers: LCCN 2016052714 (print) | LCCN 2017002211 (ebook) | ISBN 9781626176263 (hardcover : alk. paper) | ISBN 9781681033563 (ebook)
Subjects: LCSH: Balinese cat–Juvenile literature.
Classification: LCC SF449.B34 R38 2018 (print) | LCC SF449.B34 (ebook) | DDC 636.8/3–dc23
LC record available at https://lccn.loc.gov/2016052714

Editor: Nathan Sommer   Designer: Lois Stanfield

Printed in the United States of America, North Mankato, MN.

Table of Contents

Balinese are medium-sized cats with an **elegant** look.

They may look **slender**, but these cats have strong bodies.

They are known for their **silky**, medium-long fur.

plume

Balinese fur is longest around the tail. This long fur creates a fluffy **plume**.

Balinese come from
Siamese cats. Sometimes,
Siamese cats had kittens
with long hair.

United States

N
W E
S

Siamese

Balinese

In the 1950s, Americans **bred** these long-haired cats to create the Balinese **breed**!

Balinese dancers

The cats were named after the graceful dancers of Bali, Indonesia. Cat shows later helped make them popular.

Today, people still love this friendly breed!

Pointy Ears and Point Coats

Balinese have triangle-shaped heads and big, pointy ears. All have blue eyes. Their eyes are large and almond-shaped.

Balinese Profile

------ pointy ears

------ blue eyes

plumed
tail

Weight: 5 to 10 pounds (2 to 5 kilograms)

Life Span: 9 to 15 years

Balinese have **point coats**.
These coats first came in
four colors.

Balinese Coats

seal

blue

red

cream

In 2008, the breed grew to include more colors. **Seal** point is most common.

These cats have long, **athletic** bodies. They use strong legs to jump and climb.

Balinese are also **vocal** cats. They tell their owners what they want!

Balinese love to spend time with their owners. They are interested in every family activity!

They enjoy playing with other pets, too.

Balinese are a playful, **intelligent** breed. Some learn to fetch toys and treats.

These cats can even learn to walk on a leash. Balinese are always on the go!

Glossary

athletic—being strong, fit, and active

bred—purposely mated two cats to make kittens with certain qualities

breed—a type of cat

elegant—having grace and beauty

intelligent—able to learn and be trained

plume—a section of long, fluffy fur

point coats—light-colored coats with darker fur in certain areas; pointed cats have dark faces, ears, legs, and tails.

seal—very dark brown

silky—soft, smooth, and shiny

slender—thin

vocal—expressing sound often or loudly

To Learn More

AT THE LIBRARY

Felix, Rebecca. *Siamese*. Minneapolis, Minn.: Bellwether Media, 2016.

Finne, Stephanie. *Balinese Cats*. Minneapolis, Minn.: Checkerboard Library, 2015.

Sexton, Colleen. *The Life Cycle of a Cat*. Minneapolis, Minn.: Bellwether Media, 2011.

ON THE WEB

Learning more about Balinese cats is as easy as 1, 2, 3.

1. Go to www.factsurfer.com.

2. Enter "Balinese cats" into the search box.

3. Click the "Surf" button and you will see a list of related web sites.

With factsurfer.com, finding more information is just a click away.

Index

The images in this book are reproduced through the courtesy of: Gerard Lacz Images/ SuperStock, front cover, p. 8; Ardea/ Labat, Jean Michel/ Animals Animals, p. 4; Arco Images GmbH/ Alamy, pp. 4-5, 15 (upper left), 20-21; Jean Michel Labat/ ardea.com/ Pantheon/ SuperStock, p. 6; Juniors/ Juniors/ SuperStock, pp. 6-7, 8-9 (subjects); Charts and BG, pp. 8-9 (background); paul kennedy/ Alamy, p. 10; Juniors Bildarchiv GmbH/ Alamy, pp. 11, 14-15, 15 (lower right), 19 (subjects); Tierfotoagentur/ Alamy, pp. 12-13 (subject), 15 (upper right), 17 (subject); BLUR LIFE 1975, pp. 12-13, 17 (background); Helmi Flick/ Helmi Flick Cat Photography, pp. 13, 16; Monika Wroblewska/ Shutterstock, p. 15 (lower left); BravissimoS, pp. 18-19 (subjects); zhu difeng, pp. 18-19 (background); Efired, p. 19 (background); mauritius images GmbH/ Alamy, p. 20.